CW01025176

To God on a Magic Carpet

Meditating with Children

by Sister Anthony

Spectrum Publications

I would like to thank the worldwide Congregation of the Sisters of Nazareth for providing me with opportunities to develop my prayer life and for encouraging me to use my talents.

Always my heartfelt thanks for the support of my parents, brother and sister.

John Coleman, Religious Education Consultant for the Geraldton Diocese who encouraged and assisted me in so many ways.

Maria Rohr, Spectrum Publications whose enthusiasm is infectious!

First Published in Australia in 2004
Reprinted 2008
by Spectrum Publications Pty Ltd
PO Box 75, Richmond, Vic. 312
Telephone: +61(3) 9415 9750, Facsimile: +61(3) 9419 0783
e-mail: spectrum@spectrumpublications.com.au
web: www.spectrumpublications.com.au

Design: Kelly Drinkwater
Illustrations: Mike Drinkwater
Typeface: Garnet

ISBN 0 86786 359 5

*To all the children who have
enriched my life and taught me
so much about prayer.*

Contents

Magic Carpet

Foreword

'I would go behind my bed into an empty space that was easy to close off with a curtain....and there I used to think. I understand now that I was meditating without knowing it and that God was really instructing me.'

These words from the autobiography of St Therese of Lisieux refer to the days when, deemed too young to attend Church services, the little Therese entered into a relationship with God which deepened and grew as she matured.

For many years I have been praying with children using the traditional prayers we all know and love so much as the 'Our Father' and 'Hail Mary'. But that quotation from St Therese set me thinking. In today's world children are bombarded with noise from all sides. They have little opportunity to find a place of quiet to sit and think.

Yet children are natural contemplatives. One need only think of a child's openness to awe and wonder: their delight in creation as they observe a starlit night, wild flowers and birds singing.

This sense of joyous wonder has often been dulled in adults, too busy to Stop! Look! Listen!

The television, computer, Walkman radio etc have all conspired to disrupt the natural rhythms of the universe so in tune with that of the child.

It was this realisation that led me to create, 'pools of stillness' in the school day giving the children and myself time to sit, reflect and listen, gradually becoming aware of a loving Presence very close to each one of us.

Children love new words so I introduced the word *'meditation'* rather than prayer not wanting any pre-conceived ideas to intrude on what, for many, was a new experience.

We began very simply by sitting still and listening. (Those who know young children will realise that this is a major feat)! Perseverance and initially very short periods (I tried two minutes) pay dividends.

'But this isn't prayer,' I can hear some object. On the contrary, I believe it is. Many of us would benefit from a quiet listening session since most (including myself) spend too much time talking! Let's give God a chance to talk!

At this point, I'd like to say it is very important that you practise these activities yourself. 'Don't talk about it - experience it,' say the mystics of all the traditions.

The children I have the privilege to work with have told me how much this form of prayer appeals to them. (I include some of their remarks as footnotes).

Timing

I realise that catechists, seeing children on a weekly basis, are in a very different setting to the class teacher. Nevertheless, I would urge all to start and leave spaces for the Holy Spirit to work.

The pace or order in which you proceed depends very much on the group. Some children respond eagerly and will cooperate fully others less so. Each section should be undertaken for at least four sessions (more if need be).

Where you stop depends on the children. Some love 'The Lift' others 'The Magic Carpet'. Let them dictate the pace making sure that the quiet individual at the back is heard!.

The pauses are indicated in some areas only. If you meditate alongside the children the pauses will come naturally.

One word of caution! Ten minutes is long enough for young children. If they need a longer spell they will imitate St Therese and find a quiet place.

Music

I haven't mentioned the use of music to help create a relaxed atmosphere. There are probably many good C.D's and cassettes on the market though I think these are probably more helpful to adults.

Children's imaginations are more alive than ours so they need fewer 'props'.

Sitting

I have found it helpful, in order to reduce embarrassed giggling at the early stages, that the children should be seated facing the teacher or catechist. Later, you may have them seated in a circle on the floor around lighted candles, an open Bible, crucifix or whatever is appropriate.

'I do my meditation in the back of the car.'
(Andrew 10 years)

'My cousin couldn't sleep so I taught her to meditate
and she soon dozed off.'
(Hannah 8 years)

'I take my little brother to the bedroom and teach him
to meditate. Mum likes it.'
(Joanne 9 years)

'If I feel stressed I meditate for five minutes.'
(Michelle 14 years)

Age Groups

Which age groups should take part?

I have used these exercises with Year 1-7 and all have reacted enthusiastically. I say all but you do get the child who remarks, "I feel as if I am going into a black hole!" In such cases I generally remark, "Well just sit and think about your birthday!"

I have mentioned children's comments. This is a sensitive area. Some children are eager to share their experiences with the group, others very reluctant. Respect their privacy.

You may suggest the keeping of a 'Prayer Journal,' where they can record meaningful experiences in drawing or writing.

From the beginning it is vital to call on the help of the Holy Spirit who is the prime mover in all of this. Entrust the children to Him.

If you persevere you will notice your attitudes changing as you become more aware of the 'Divine Presence' in your life.

"... the Lord was not in the fire - and after the fire there was the soft whisper of a voice. When Elijah heard it he covered his face".

(1 Kings 19:12-13)

Listening

Aim - to bring stillness

Sitting

1. Everyone sit facing me. Sit upright, your back resting against the chair. Put your feet on the floor slightly apart.

    Hands are resting gently on your lap.

    Rest one on top of the other.

    Close or lower your eyes.

Listening

2. Listen to the sounds outside the room. (15 seconds)

3. Listen to the sounds inside the room. (15 seconds)

4. After I count three slowly open your eyes. 1   2   3

    > 'I didn't know the classroom clock ticked.'
    > *(Ryan 9 years)*

Awareness

Aim - to become aware of the sensations in your body

Sitting

1. Everyone sit facing me. Sit upright, your back resting against
    the chair. Put your feet on the floor slightly apart.

    Hands are resting gently on your lap.

    Rest one on top of the other.

    Close or lower your eyes.

Listening

2. Listen to the sounds outside the room. (15 seconds)

3. Listen to the sounds inside the room. (15 seconds)

4. Read the following slowly pausing after each word:

Become aware of the feelings in the:
- top of your head
- tongue
- eyes
- lips
- cheeks
- jaw
- neck
- shoulders
- arms
- hands
- back
- hips
- legs
- feet

5. Repeat the list again.

6. Now repeat it quietly to yourself.

7. Listen to the sounds outside the room. (15 seconds)

8. Listen to the sounds inside the room. (15 seconds)

9. After I count three slowly open your eyes. 1   2   3

'I felt totally relaxed. In fact I nearly fell asleep.'
(Katy 9 years)

Breathing 1

Aim - to become aware of your breath

Sitting

1. Everyone sit facing me. Sit upright, your back resting against the chair. Put your feet on the floor slightly apart.

   Hands are resting gently on your lap.

   Rest one on top of the other.

   Close or lower your eyes.

Listening

2. Listen to the sounds outside the room. (15 seconds)

3. Listen to the sounds inside the room. (15 seconds)

Awareness

4. Become aware that you are breathing. (30 seconds)

5. Notice the gentle rise and fall of your chest as you breathe in and out. (30 seconds)

6. Listen to the sounds outside the room. (15 seconds)

7. Listen to the sounds inside the room. (15 seconds)

8. After I count three open your eyes.   1   2   3

'No problem at all with this.'
(Peter 9 years)

Breathing 2

Aim - to become aware of your breath

Sitting

1. Everyone sit facing me. Sit upright, your back resting against the chair. Put your feet on the floor slightly apart.

   Hands are resting gently on your lap.

   Rest one on top of the other.

   Close or lower your eyes.

Listening

2. Listen to the sounds outside the room. (15 seconds)

3. Listen to the sounds inside the room. (15 seconds)

Awareness

4. Become aware that you are breathing. (30 seconds)

5. Notice the gentle rise and fall of your chest as you breathe in and out. (30 seconds)

6. As you breathe in, imagine you are taking in the power and love of God. (1 minute)

7. As you breathe out, imagine you are breathing out all your worries and troubles. (1 minute)

8. Listen to the sounds outside the room. (15 seconds)

9. Listen to the sounds inside the room. (15 seconds)

10. After I count three open your eyes. 1   2   3

Visualisation 1

Inviting the Sun
Aim - to become aware that I am loved by God

1. Sitting

2. Listening

3. Visualisation

4. Imagine that you are lying in a field full of flowers. The sun is shining from a blue sky. Birds are singing. There is no one else there just you. (1 minute)

5. Feel the sun pouring its warmth into your body.
    You are feeling warm and relaxed. (1 minute)

6. Realise that God, your loving Father, has created the sun for you.

    The rays of the sun are bringing God's love to you.
    Feel that love filling up every part of you. (1 minute)

7. You are totally accepted just as you are. You don't need to do anything. You are totally loved.

8. Enjoy basking in the sun filled up with God's love. (2 minutes)

9. Listen.

10. Open your eyes. 1 2 3

    'That was amazing.
    I could have stayed forever.'
    (Natasha 9 years)

Visualisation 2

Meeting Jesus
Aim - to become aware of Jesus' presence

1. Sitting

2. Listening

3. Visualisation

4. Imagine you are walking along a beach. (pause)
   The sand is soft and warm on your bare feet. (pause)
   Little waves come lapping round your ankles. The water is
   warm. (pause)

5. Walk along enjoying the sun, sea and sand. (pause)
   In the distance you see someone. He waves. You realise it
   is Jesus. (pause)

6. You feel happy. Jesus wants to meet you.
   He is almost beside you. See, He has found a lovely shell.
   He gives it to you. Can you hear the sea in it? (pause)

7. Together you walk along the shore. Is there something you
   want to tell Him? (pause)

8. Maybe He has something to tell you. (pause)
   Perhaps there's nothing special, so just enjoy being with
   Jesus your best friend. (pause)

9. It's time to go.
   Say goodbye.

10. Walk slowly back
    along the beach.
    Jesus waves to you.
    Wave back. (pause)

11. Listen.

12. Open your eyes. 1   2   3

Mantra

Aim - to become aware of God's indwelling through repetition of a word or phrase

1. Explanation

When you were little you could not speak many words. Probably the first words you said were, 'Mama', 'Dada'.

Once you learned these words you kept repeating them over and over. Do you think your parents tired of hearing them? Of course not. They knew you were beginning to communicate with them.

In the same way God our Father, loves to hear us utter a word or words that mean a great deal. Take for instance the words of Jesus, "Do not be afraid." Jesus said that many times yet we can get scared like the disciples and forget Jesus is there to help us.

We are going to repeat that phrase over and over until we realise it is true.

We don't need to be afraid.

Imagine you hear Jesus saying it. Repeating the same word over and over is called a mantra. This form of prayer is used by many great religions of the world.

Let's begin.

2. Sitting

3. Listening

4. Become conscious of your breath.

5. As you breathe in say, "Do not …"
    As you breathe out finish the sentence, "be afraid"

6. Do not - be afraid.

7. Repeat 10 times.

8. Listen.

9. Open your eyes. 1   2   3

10. You may use these words or word:

    - Jesus

    - Peace

    - Jesus, You are always with me.

'It makes you feel peaceful.'
(Daniel 10 years)

The Lift 1

Aim - to be come conscious of the Indwelling of God (part 1)

1. Sitting

2. Listening

3. In front of you is a lift.
    Press the button to open the door.
    Step inside.
    Press the button again. The lift moves down.
    You have arrived.
    Step out of the lift.

4. In front of you is a door.
    Put your hand in your pocket and take out a key.
    (You alone can open the door)

5. The door opens and you enter an empty room.

6. There is a large window looking out on a garden, beach,
    lake, mountain or whatever you wish.

7. You can now start decorating your room.
    You just need to wish and it happens.
    Think of carpets, chairs, beanbags, curtains etc

8. If you want a pet you can have a cat, dog or both.

9. Now your room is ready.
    Open the glass doors leading outside.
    Take a deep breath and enjoy the fresh air.

10. It's time to go so come inside, close the door.
    You are not sad because you can return anytime you wish.

11. This room is inside your heart.
    It is part of you.

12. Lock the door.
    Open the lift.
    Go up.
    Step outside.

13. Listen.

14. Open your eyes.   1   2   3

> 'Can I draw my room?'
> *(Martyn 9 years)*

The Lift 2

Aim - to become aware of the Indwelling of God (part 2)

1. Sitting

2. Listening

3. You are standing outside the lift.
   Press the button to open the door.
   Step inside.
   Press the button again. The lift moves down.
   You have arrived. Step inside your special room.
   Remember how the room looked on your last visit.

4. Do you want to lie in front of the fire or stretch on your bean bag? (pause)

   You feel really happy. (pause)
   Enjoy the safe feeling. (pause)

5. There is a knock at the door.

6. Open it.

7. Jesus is there.

8. Invite Him in.

9. Where will you sit?
   Invite Jesus to share your beanbag.
   Maybe you want to go for a walk, ride or a swim. (pause)

10. Jesus is so glad to be with you. He laughs at the funny story you tell Him. He is concerned at your sad news. (pause)

11. Tell Him about anything that interests you:
    - your family
    - school
    - hobbies
    - worries

12. Listen to Him.

13. It is time to go.

14. Say goodbye to Jesus.

15. Enter the lift.
    Return to the surface.

16. Listen.

17. Open your eyes.   1   2   3

> 'I told Jesus He could stay.
> Jesus and me planned to go swimming next time.'
> *(Danielle 9 years)*

Magic Carpet

Aim - A Visit to Mary

1. Sitting

2. Listening

3. In front of you is a carpet of brilliant colours. When you sit on it you say a magic word that makes it rise through the air. Think of a word. (pause)

4. Sit on the carpet and say the magic word, which only you know.

5. The carpet is rising.

6. It moves through the air gathering speed rising higher and higher.

7. You are whizzing over mountains, seas, rivers and cities.

8. You are now in a country where the sky is very blue. The sun is shining. Below you is a little white walled town.

9. The carpet descends and reaches the ground.

10. Step off and roll up your carpet placing it behind a palm tree.

Part 2

1. You see an archway in the wall. Walk through it.
   A little way up the street a young woman is sweeping the street in front of a white washed house. She waves to you. You realise it is Mary. She looks so happy to see you. (pause)

2. Mary sees you are hot after your journey and invites you to sit on the bench outside the house.
   She goes inside to fetch some lemonade and returns with a cool drink for both of you. (pause)

3. You sit with Mary on the bench sipping your drinks. She tells you about the visit of the angel and how happy she is to be carrying God's son, Jesus.
   She places your hands on her stomach. You can feel the baby kicking inside. (pause)

4. Realise that this growing baby is Jesus who will give his life for you. Tell Mary how much you want to love her son and ask her to help you. (pause)

5. It is time to go.
   Say goodbye.
   Walk towards the archway.
   Turn and wave.

6. Find your carpet.
   Say your magic word.
   The carpet rises and moves swiftly through the air.

7. Return home to this room.

8. Listen.

9. Open your eyes. 1   2   3

'I actually felt the
baby kicking!'
(Katrina 9 years)

Magic Carpet

Aim - A visit to Bethlehem

1. Sitting

2. Listening

3. Unroll your carpet.
    Sit on it.
    Say your magic word.

4. The carpet is rising.

5. You are moving swiftly over mountains, seas, rivers and cities.

6. You slow down over a white walled city.
    It is dark and the sky is full of stars.
    The carpet descends.

7. You land outside the walls.
    Hide the carpet.

8. Walk through the gateway in the walls.
    There is a lot of noise and bustle in the streets - lights shine from all the houses.

9. Walk behind a rather poor looking motel.
    You see a light coming from a barn.
    Move towards it.

10. Knock at the door and enter.

11. The place is lit by a lamp.
    You see it is a stable.
    A donkey and a cow are standing quietly.
    A woman is lying on a heap of straw holding a baby.
    Her husband invites you to come nearer.
    You realise it's Mary. (pause)

12. She recognises you and smiles - calling you by name.
    You kneel beside her and gaze at the baby - it's Jesus. (pause)

13. Mary asks you if you want to hold Him. Hold out your arms.
    Feel the weight of the newborn baby. (pause)

14. He laughs up at you.
    How are you feeling?
    Tell Him what is in your heart. (pause)

15. Hand Him back very carefully.
    You are filled with happiness. Mary and Joseph thank you for
    coming. (pause)

16. It is time to go.
    Say goodbye.
    Give a final wave at the door.

17. Move back through the crowds.
    They are unaware of the great event that is taking place in
    their midst.

18. Feel Jesus with you.
    He loves you for taking time to be with Him.
    Find your carpet.
    Say your word.

19. Return home to this room.

20. Listen.

21. Open your eyes. 1   2   3

    'I nearly cried
    when Mary let
    me hold Jesus.'
    (*Christina 10 years*)

Magic Carpet

Aim - A visit to Joseph

1. Sitting

2. Listening

3. Unroll your carpet.
   Sit on it.
   Say your magic word.

4. The carpet is rising. You are moving swiftly over mountains, seas, rivers and cities.
   You descend slowly.
   Step off.
   Roll up your carpet and put it behind a palm tree.

5. In front of you is a little village. Follow the dusty track that leads you to the main street. As you walk along the narrow street between white washed houses a boy, about your own age runs out. He recognises you.
   It's Jesus. (pause)

6. He's delighted to see you and asks you to come home with him.
   Mary is cleaning up but stops to welcome you as you enter the house.
   You walk through the house and find yourself in a sort of outdoor workshop. Look around. What do you see? (pause)

7. Joseph, a big strong man is making a chair. He too smiles at you as you enter.
   Jesus asks him for off-cuts of wood so that you can both make something.
   Joseph fills a box with wood, nails, glue and a hammer. He warns you both to be careful. (pause)

8. You feel quite at home in the presence of this quiet, friendly man. (pause)

9. Sit on the warm sandy floor.
   What are you going to make?
   Discuss it with Jesus.
   Feel the wood in your hand. (pause)

10. Jesus has started. You had better hurry up and begin. (pause)
    You have both finished. Jesus laughs at his toy. It's a bit rough.
    He looks at yours. What does he say? (pause)

11. Now show what you have made to Joseph. (pause)
    He admires your work.
    Hear him call your name and tell you how good you are.
    (pause)

12. Mary calls everyone to come and have cakes and a drink.
    You can sit where you want to.

13. Just enjoy being with this happy family who belong to your
    family also. (pause)

14. It is time to go.
    Jesus walks down the road with you.
    Mary and Joseph stand at the door waving.
    Hear Jesus telling you how happy he is to live with Joseph
    and Mary. (pause)

15. Find your carpet.
    Say your magic word.
    Return home.

16. Listen

17. Open your eyes.
    1   2   3

    'I showed Jesus how to
    make an aeroplane.
    He'd never seen one!'
    (Diarmuid 9 years)

23

Magic Carpet

Aim - A Visit to Zacchaeus

1. Sitting

2. Listening

3. Unroll your carpet.
   Sit on it.
   Say your magic word.

4. The carpet is rising.
   You move through the air over mountains, seas, rivers
   and cities.

5. You reach a warm country of blue skies.
   The carpet descends.
   You are outside the wall of a city.
   Put your carpet behind a palm tree.

6. A large crowd is going through the archway. You hear people
   say, "Jesus is coming."

7. Crowds of people are lining the streets buzzing with excitement.

8. You are under a large sycamore tree.
   Crowds of people are looking up into the tree shaking their fists
   and jeering.
   A little man perched amongst the branches looks down
   anxiously. What is he doing up there?
   It is Zacchaeus, the tax collector, a cheat and a thief. (pause)

9. Suddenly the name calling stops.
   People were so occupied with Zacchaeus they didn't notice
   Jesus walking amongst them.

10. He stops under the tree and looks up.
    "Zacchaeus, come down, I want to have a meal with you."
    Zacchaeus, filled with joy, is scrambling down.
    Jesus puts his arm around his shoulders. (pause)

11. This is awful. Surely Jesus knows what a bad man Zacchaeus is?
People start muttering, "It's not fair. Why doesn't He visit my house?"
You join in the grumbles. (pause)

12. Jesus looks right at you and says your name -
"I love you too but Zacchaeus needs help badly:
Can't you be glad that he is trying to change?" (pause)

13. How do you feel right now? (pause)
Jesus takes your hand. Together you walk into the house of Zacchaeus.

14. You are thinking of the things in your life you need to change.
Your attitude to:
- your parents
- brothers and sisters
- teachers
- friends (pause)

15. Tell Jesus you do want to change.
Hear Him promise to help. (pause)

16. It's time to go.
See Zacchaeus' happy face as he asks Jesus to sit down.
Tell him you're glad for him. (pause)

17. Find your carpet.
Sit on it.
Return home to this room.

18. Listen.

19. Open your eyes. 1   2   3

'Jesus is as good as a psychotherapist any day!'
(Charles 7 years)

Postscript

When discussing these forms of prayer with colleagues some demurred at the use of the word 'magic' when linked with prayer.

While understanding this reaction, I feel in this case there should not be a problem.

Most children have heard stories involving magic carpets as a means of travel. If, when introducing this form of prayer (incidentally encouraged by Saint Ignatius of Loyola) you mention that we are going to use our God given imagination to visit Jesus in the gospel stories, or in his home, the carpet mode of transport seems perfectly viable and one which the children love.

You can of course devise another method of transport or 'jump right into the scenes'.

However you get there, it is the meeting with Jesus, which is important!

' I felt really nervous during an exam. Then I remembered our
five-minute meditations. I put my pen down and started.
Afterwards I felt really calm and got on with the paper.'
(Verity 13 years)